Dysconnected

Humans Isolated by their Personal Technology

A Book by Anton Scamvougeras

Vancouver
2016

Acknowledgments are due to family, friends, and colleagues who have wittingly or unwittingly encouraged or inspired this endeavour. In particular, thanks to Linda Chapman, Kathy Jordan, Gary Jordan, Henry Symonds, Kent Sutherland, Roger Frie, Peter Skippen, Colin Cash, Margaret MacKinnon-Cash, Emily Marden, Michele Genge, Christine Genge, Peter Uys, Rick Taylor, Leon Berzen, Michael Abelman, Matt Beirness, Gillian Brangham, Jackie Sabourin, Tayler Theaker, Kitty Blandy, Karen Andersen, David Bain, Jim Bovard, Greg Cassap, Rob Gritten, Tim Hunt, Gord MacDonald, Arthur Mills, James Schmidt, Karl Gedlicka, Gagan Gaind, Michael Rattray, Michael Schacht, Jim Thorne, Iris Stoffberg, and Kosta & Alvina Scamvougeras.

References, attributions, illustration titles, and a concentrated collection of 'Phone Facts' appear at the back of the book.

The author can be contacted at: dysconnected1@gmail.com

Copies of the book can be obtained at: dysconnected.com

Published by AJKS Publishing, Vancouver.
Printed and Bound in Canada by Art Bookbindery, Winnipeg.

ISBN 978-0-9952056-0-4 Soft Cover

First Edition First Printing

Illustrations and cover design by Anton Scamvougeras Cover Photo by Adam Scamvougeras

This book is dedicated, with much love, and thanks,
to Margot, Adam, Jacob, and Kate.

dys- (prefix) bad, ill, abnormal;

as in: dysfunctional, dysphoric, dystopian

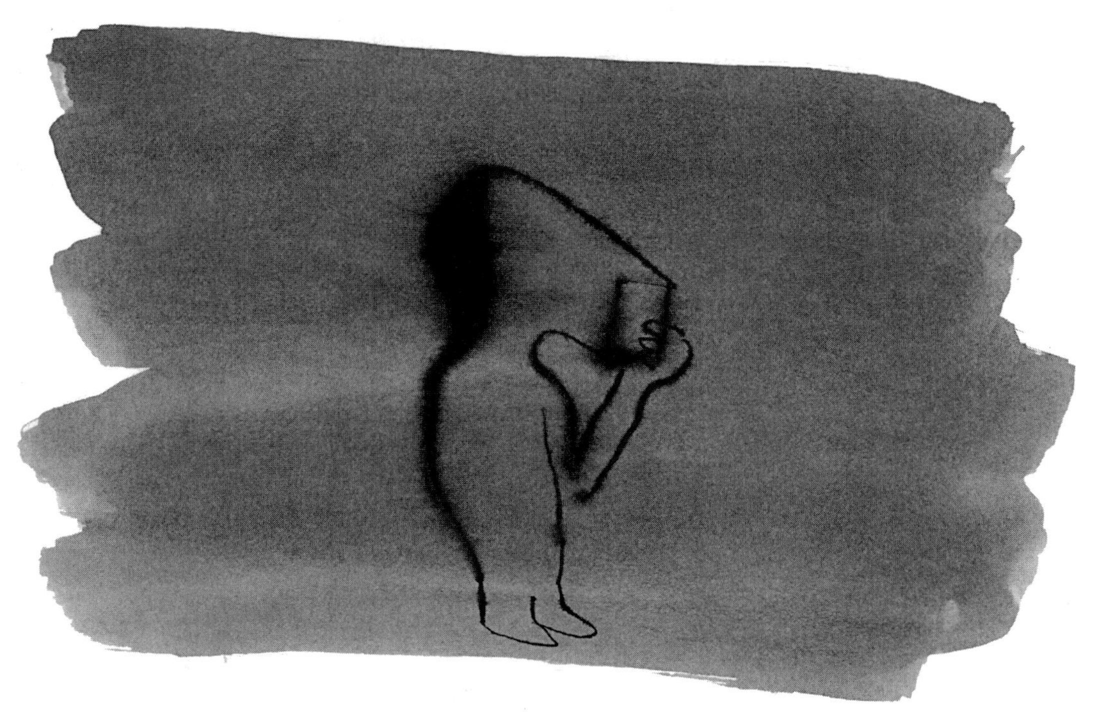

Introduction

Here's a wild idea: In the future, the happiest, most content and satisfied people will be those of us who learn to best manage our relationships with our own technological devices.

We all know how useful, powerful, and delightful our cell phones or tablets can be, but a growing number of us also have a sense that there's something potentially disturbing about the way they have so rapidly taken up such a large and central space in our lives.

Surfing, clicking, texting, sharing, friending, and liking have arguably taken the place of looking, seeing, listening, talking, thinking, and just plain doing nothing, hanging out, or being bored.

Are we losing the capacity for quiet solitude? Are we filling all previously-empty spaces in our days with electronic 'busy-ness'? Have online 'friends' taken the place of the other sort? Have second lives replaced our first? And, if this is the case, should it be cause for any concern?

'Dysconnected' is a series of pen and ink drawings that encourages us to consider the way we use our mobile devices. The images are presented alongside ideas, opinions, and facts, from various sources, with the intention of stimulating reflection.

To shape our futures for the better, we must first be aware of what we are doing in the present. This book encourages us to be mindful of how we use our devices, and to use them to improve rather than intrude upon our lives.

AS 2016

"I find myself seeing the world through a screen and not my eyes."

Ed Sheeran, singer-songwriter

aS

"We are fearful that we might be missing something;
we're probably not."

Robert Hughes, art critic

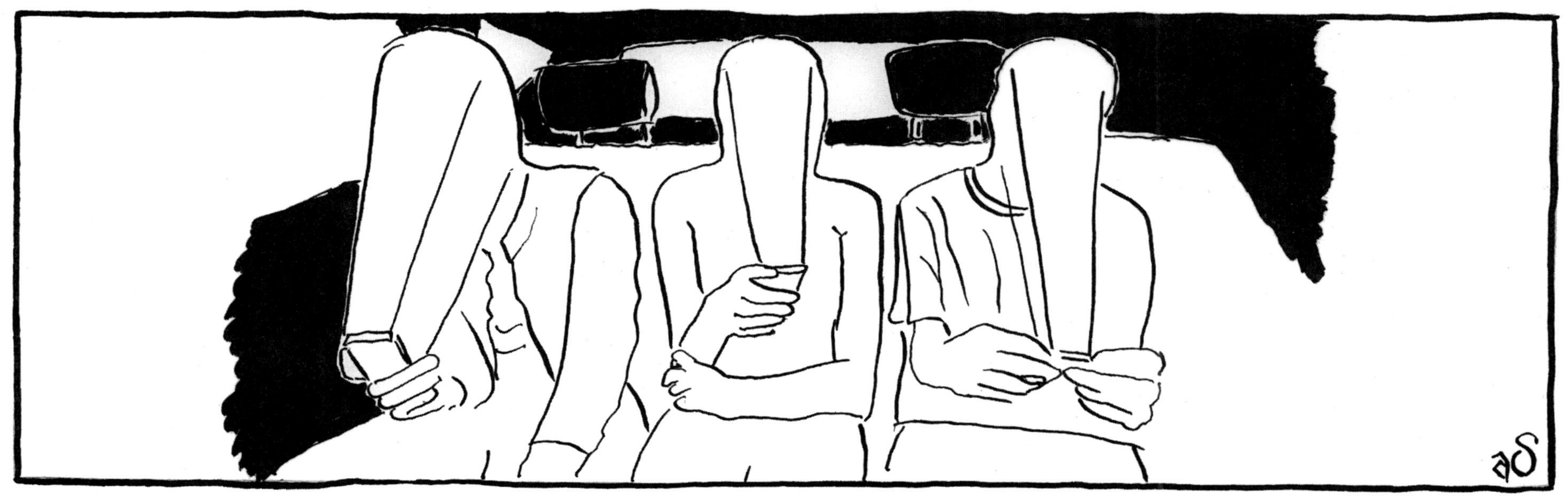

"It's easier to desire and pursue the attention of tens of millions of total strangers than it is to accept the love and loyalty of the people closest to us."

William Gibson, author, in the novel 'Idoru'

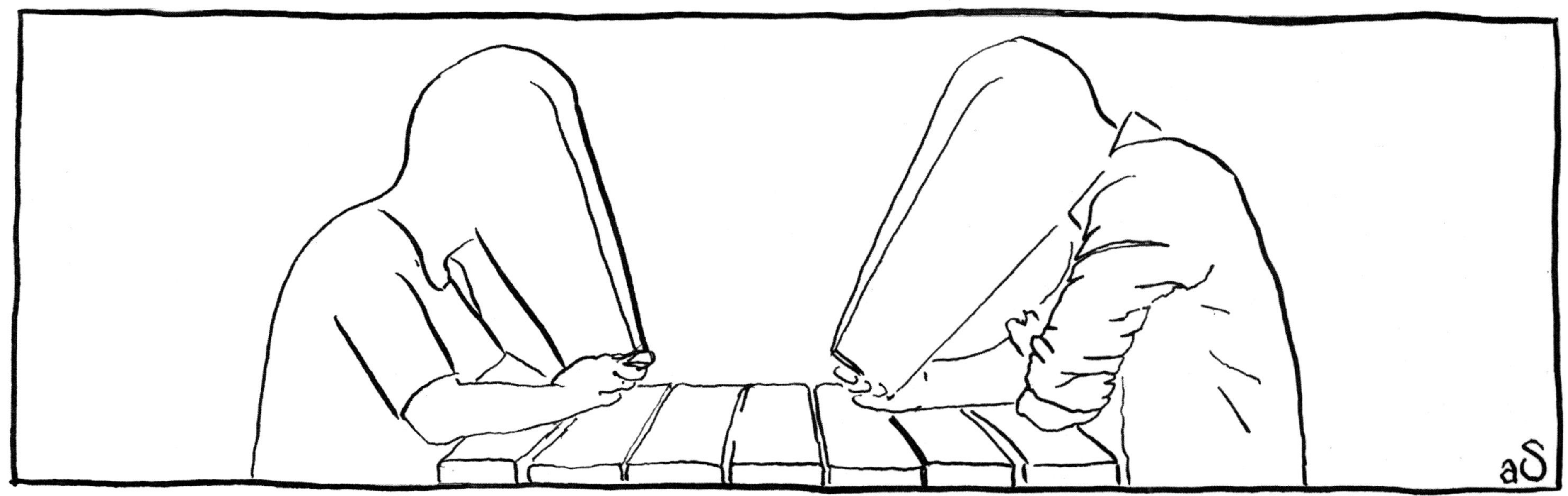

"The great myth of our times is that technology is communication."

Libby Larsen, American composer

aS

"We clutch phones to show that we do know at least one other person -- that we might look solitary but we have connections."

Margaret Heffernan, author

“Could you stop filming me?
Because I’m really here, in real life.
Enjoy it in real life rather than through your camera.”

Adele, singer, at a concert in Verona, Italy, May 2016

Pairs of strangers who got to know one another in the presence of a mobile phone felt less closeness, trust, empathy and understanding, than those who shared a conversation without a mobile phone present.

from research by sociologists Andrew Przybylski & Netta Weinstein

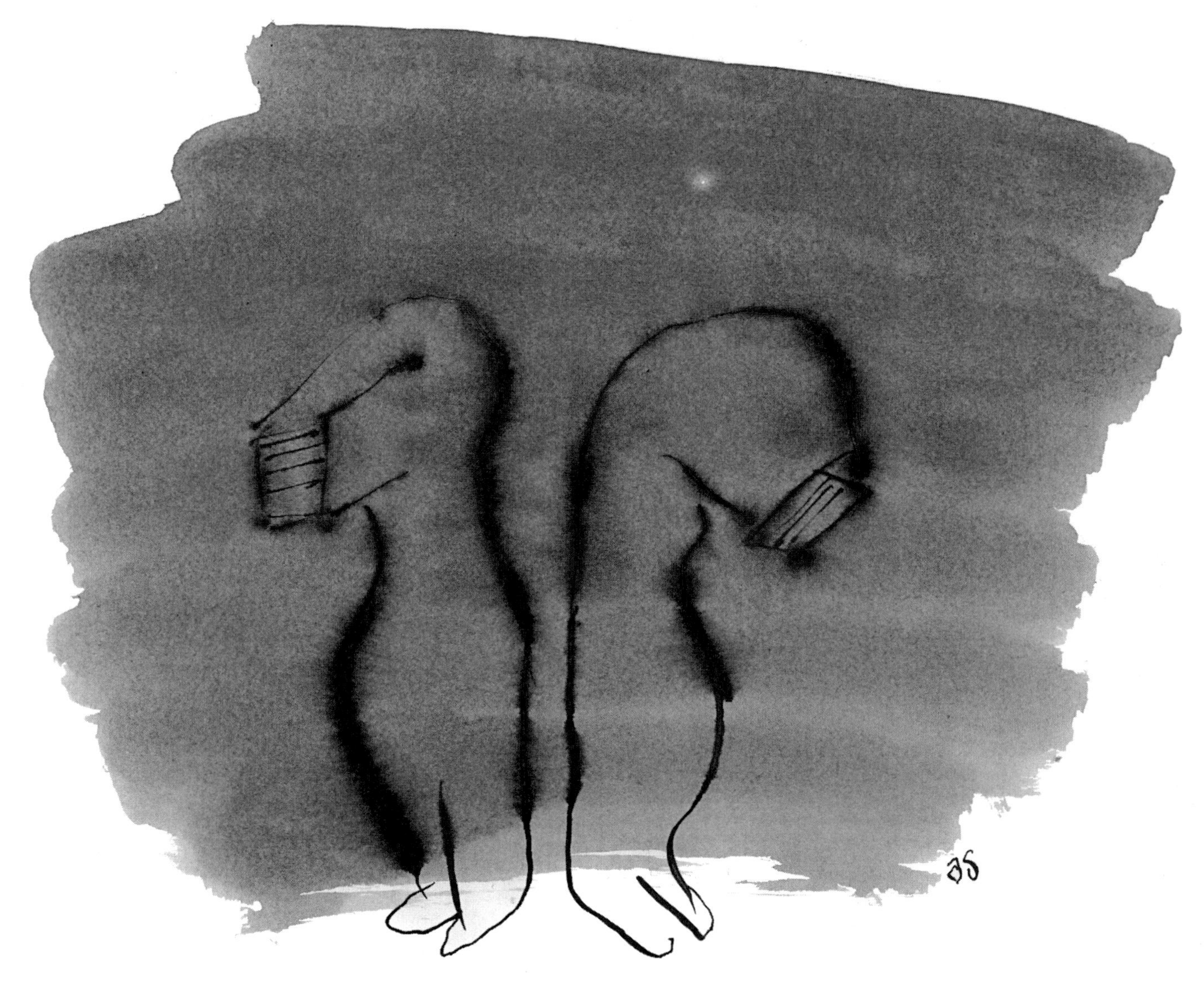

"The more time we spend interconnected via a myriad of devices, the less time we have left to develop true friendships in the real world."

Alex Morritt, author

"We are lonely but fearful of intimacy.
Digital connections may offer the illusion of companionship without the demands of friendship. Our networked life allows us to hide from each other, even as we are tethered to each other. We'd rather text than talk."

Sherry Turkle, sociologist

“Even the technology that promises to unite us, divides us.”

Dan Brown, author, in the novel ‘Angels & Demons’

“The portability of the device is its beauty and its curse.”

Rick Taylor, friend

“We all fall into our habits, our routines, our ruts. They’re used quite often, consciously or unconsciously, to avoid living, to avoid doing the messy part of having relationships with other people, of dealing with a person next to us.”

Andrew Stanton, film director

"No one's forcing you to do this. You willingly tie yourself to these leashes. And you willingly become utterly socially autistic. You no longer pick up on basic human communication clues. You're at a table with three humans, all of whom are looking at you and trying to talk to you, and you're staring at a screen!"

Dave Eggers, author, in the novel 'The Circle'

“How can people not think this is changing your brain?”

Susan Greenfield, neuroscientist

"Everybody gets so much information everyday that they lose their common sense."

Gertrude Stein, author and art collector

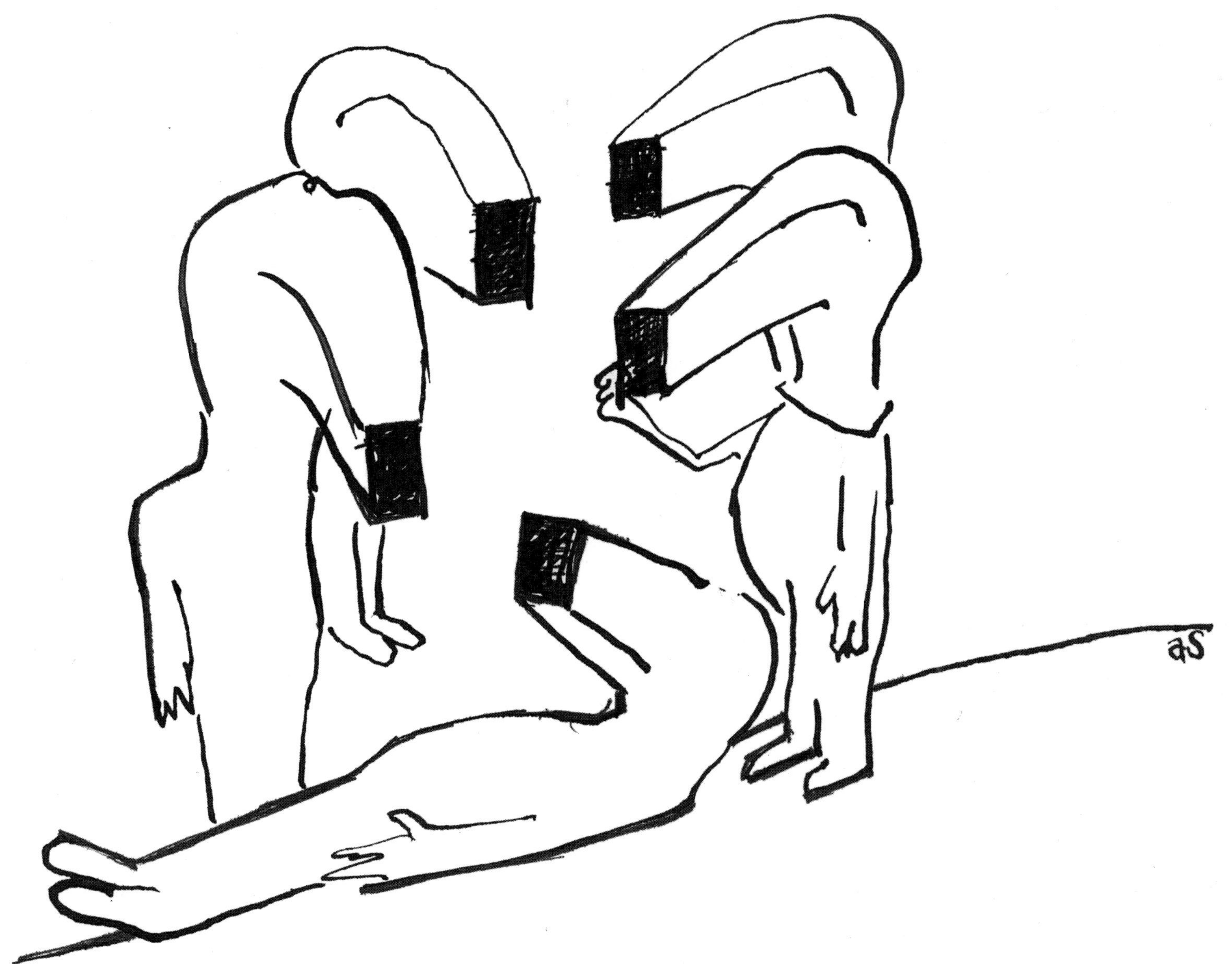
aS

“Vanity working on a weak head, produces every sort of mischief.”

Jane Austen, author, in the novel ‘Emma’

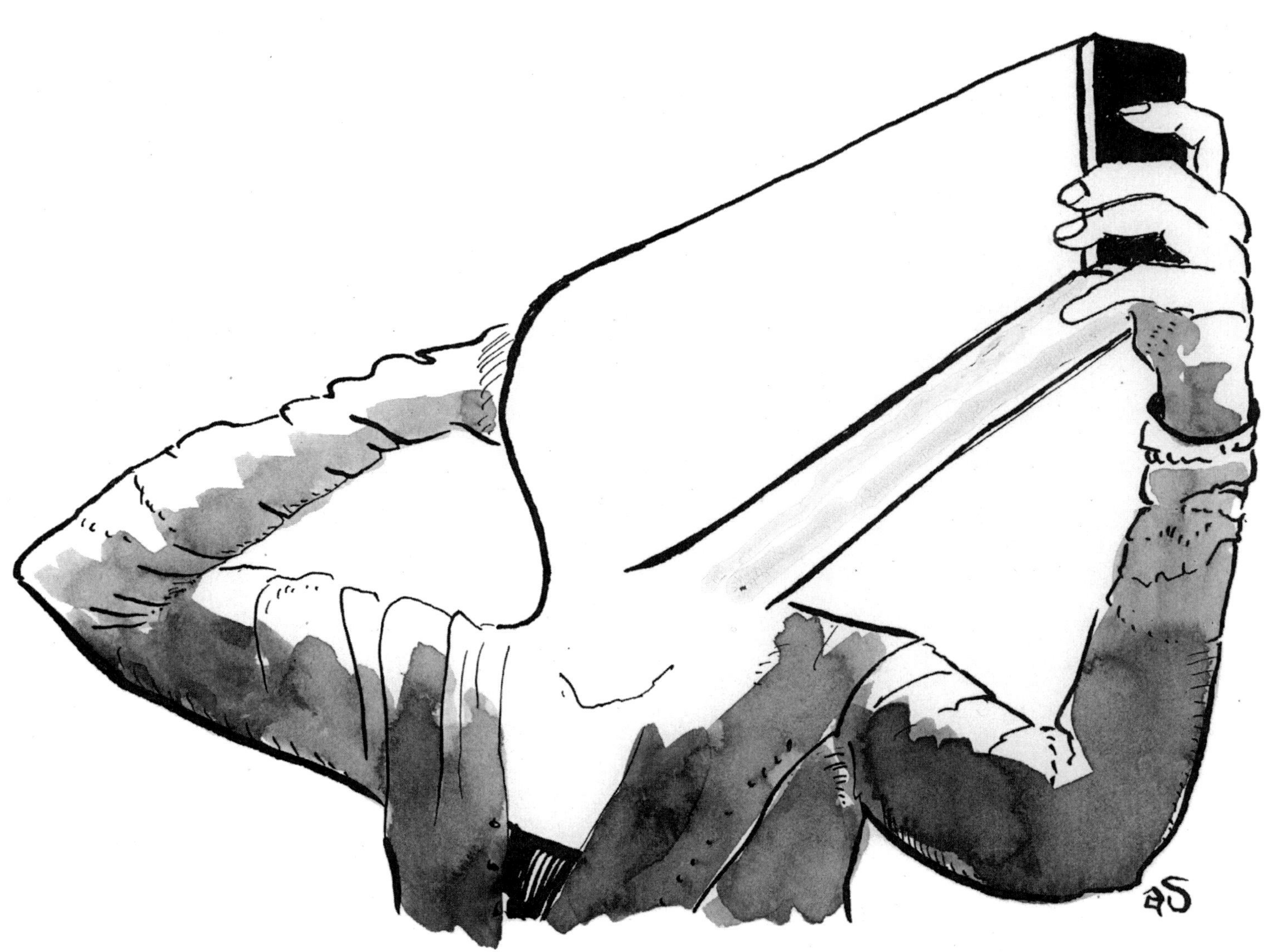

"If you truly believe you need to pick a mobile phone that "says something" about your personality, don't bother. You don't have a personality."

Charlie Brooker, satirist

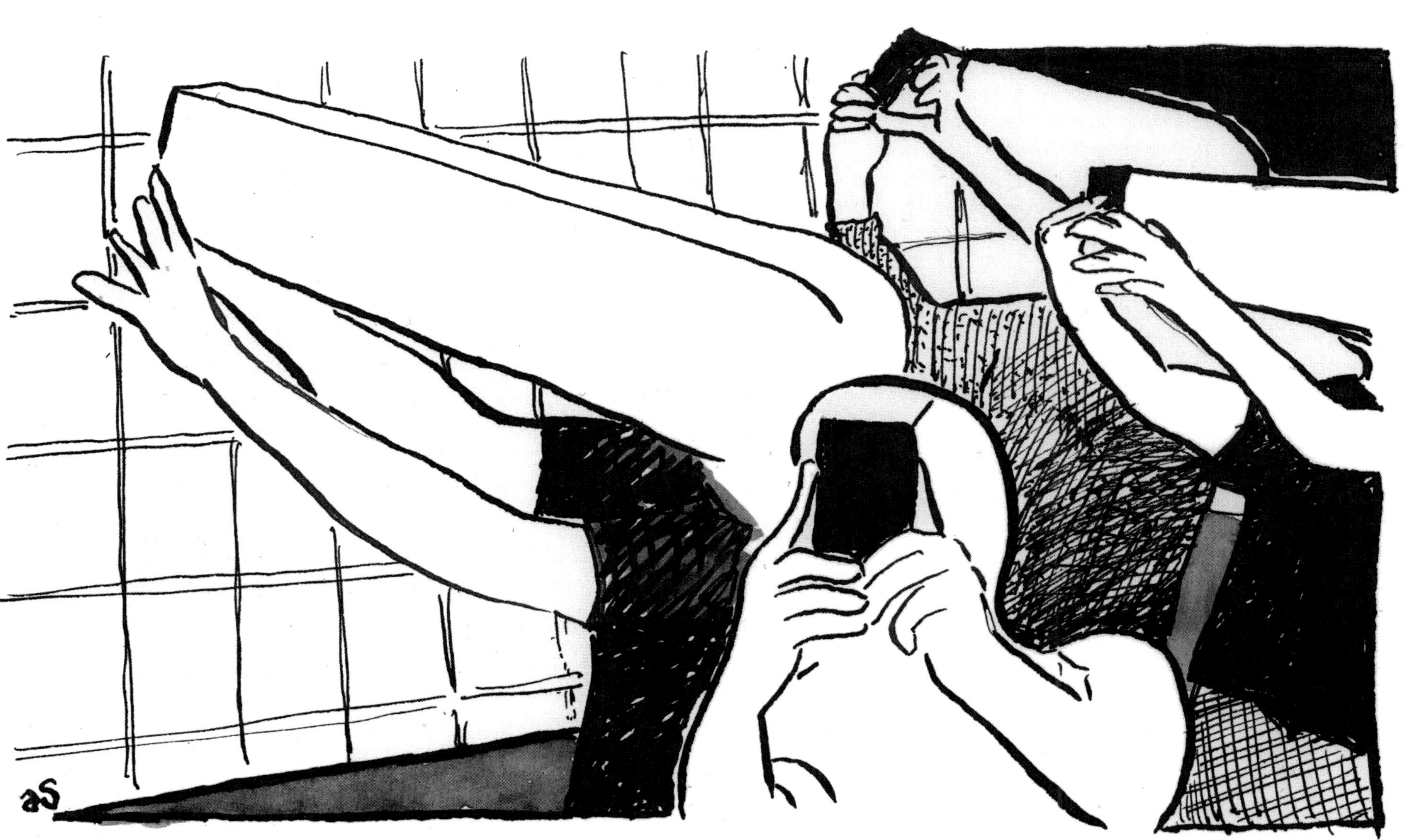

"We love ourselves more than other people,
but care more about their opinion than our own."

Marcus Aurelius, Roman emperor and philosopher

"To consider the reality of vanity, look at the peacock; it's beautiful if you look at it from the front. But if you look at it from behind, you discover the truth. Whoever gives in to such self-absorbed vanity has huge misery hiding inside them."

Pope Francis

"When Thoreau considered "where I live and what I live for," he tied together location and values. Where we live doesn't just change how we live; it informs who we become. Most recently, technology promises us lives on the screen. What values, Thoreau would ask, follow from this new location? Immersed in simulation, where do we live, and what do we live for?"

Sherry Turkle, sociologist

"The moment of drifting into thought has been clipped by modern technology. Our lives are filled with distraction with smartphones and all the rest. People are locked into not being present."

Glen Hansard, songwriter and musician

"We are a society of notoriously unhappy people
who are glad when we have killed the time
we are trying so hard to save."

Erich Fromm, humanist philosopher

aS

“If I let it, my phone easily fills up every gap in my day.”

Joe Kraus, tech sector entrepreneur

"Every time I see an adult on a bicycle,
I no longer despair for the future of the human race."

H. G. Wells, science fiction author (1866-1946),
who did not live to see a person on a bike using a cell phone

aS

“Technology… the knack of so arranging the world that we don’t have to experience it.”

Max Frisch, author, in the novel ‘Homo Faber’ (1957)

"We are what we repeatedly do."

Aristotle, philosopher,
as paraphrased by Will Durant, historian

“The center will not hold if it has been spot-welded
by an operator whose deepest concern is not with the weld
but with his lottery ticket.”

Donald Barthelme in the story “At The End Of The Mechanical Age”

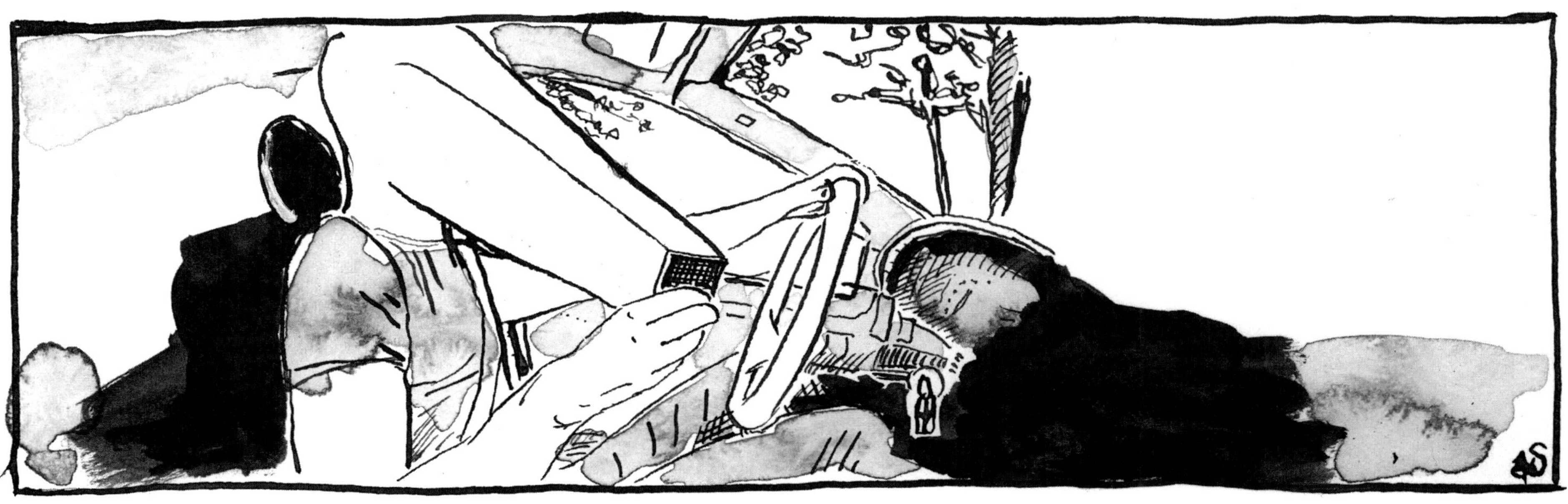

"Technology can be our best friend, and can also be the biggest party pooper of our lives. It interrupts our own story, interrupts our ability to have a thought or a daydream, to imagine something wonderful, because we're too busy bridging the walk from the cafeteria back to the office on the cell phone."

Steven Spielberg, film director

Students study for fewer than six minutes before switching to another technological distraction, such as texting or social media.

from a 2013 study by L.D. Rosen and colleagues.

"I watch for emergent technologies and pay attention to what people say they'll be good for, then see what we actually use them for. It never occurred to me that a tiny telephone with a wireless transceiver would do whatever it is that it's done to us."

William Gibson, author, inventor of the term 'cyberspace'

"It's doubtful that anyone with an internet connection at his workplace is writing good fiction."

Jonathan Franzen, author

“We shape our tools and then our tools shape us.”

Marshall McLuhan, media visionary

“If you think about some of the things that are being talked about by thoughtful, intelligent scientists, you realize that in 100 years the human race won’t even be recognizable.”

Cormac McCarthy, author of ‘The Road’.

Multi-tasking is a myth.
Humans perform most tasks one after the other.
We do tasks best when we are not distracted by other tasks.

aS

“We are exposed to more images in a day than anybody in the fourteenth century would have known in a lifetime.”

Robert Hughes, art critic

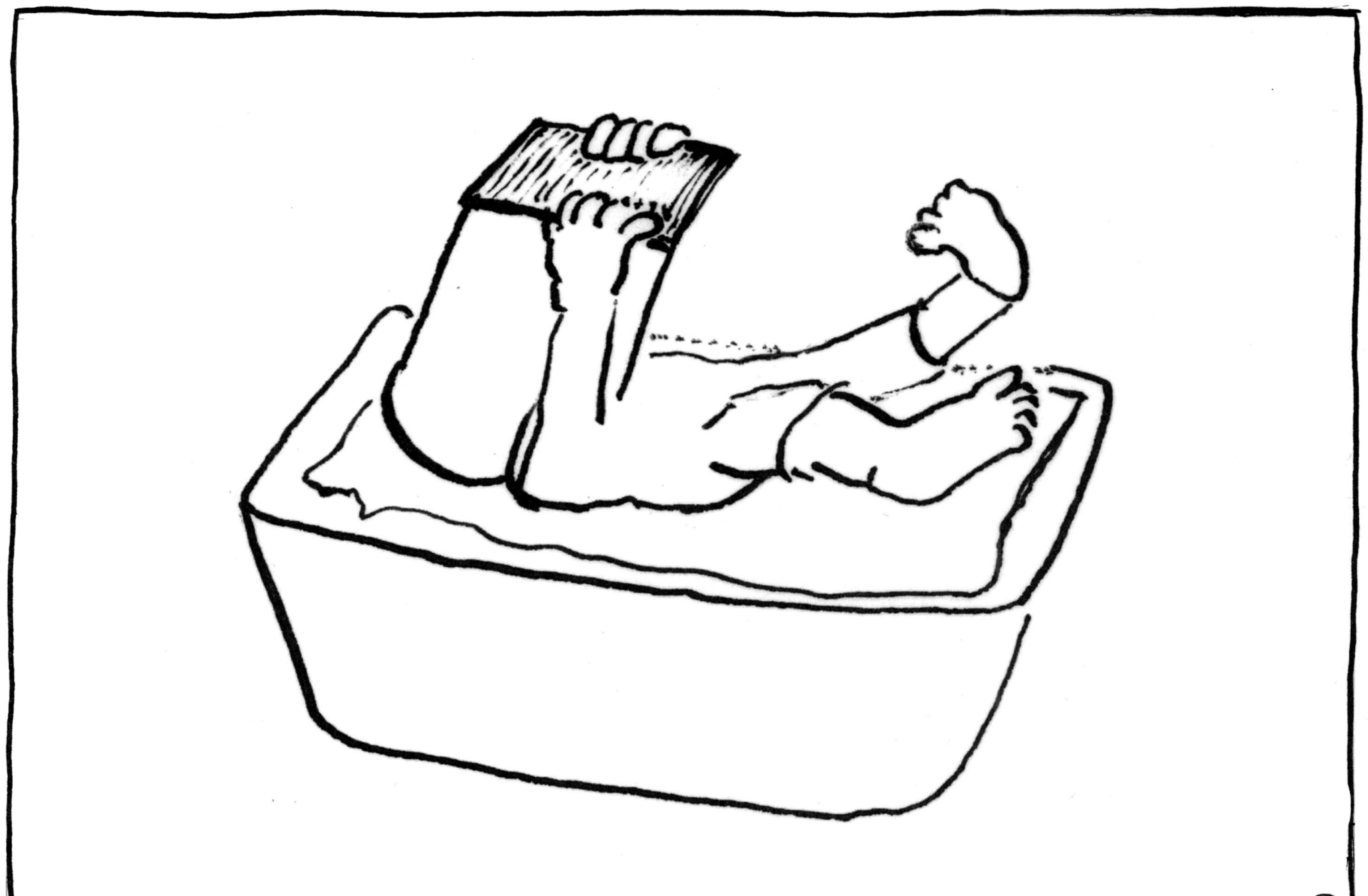

"All this modern technology just makes people try to do everything at once."

Bill Watterson, cartoonist, in the cartoon strip 'Calvin and Hobbes'

Thirty-two percent of children say they feel unimportant when their parents are distracted by their cell phones.

from research by AVG Technologies, 2015

aS

"It is unclear whether the frequency of media and technology use for adults and children is becoming a new social norm, or whether parents are underestimating the impact of media and technology on family life."

L. J. Felt & M. B. Robb in a 2016 Common Sense Media report

AS AFTER MG

"This non-stop distraction is making it impossible for the young generation to have curiosity or discipline. You need to be alone to find out anything."

Vivienne Westwood, British fashion designer

In the summer of 2009, my wife and I, and our three young children, spent two days driving across Newfoundland to a family reunion. Towards evening of the first day, I spotted a black bear foraging in the grass ahead, at the side of the quiet highway.

I alerted the family and slowly pulled the car to the shoulder. We all sat silently for a minute, hardly breathing, observing the bear. It continued to paw and nose its way through the grass, undistracted. When it started to move closer to the car, we slowly pulled away.

Early the next morning, I stood with my six year old son, Jacob, while we filled the car with gas.

"So," I asked, "what did you think of the bear?"

"It was…", he started, speaking ahead of his thoughts,

".. it was.. so.. so… ***realistic***."

"So, your kids must love the iPad?" I asked Steve Jobs, trying to change the subject. The company's first tablet was just hitting the shelves.

"They haven't used it," he told me. "We limit how much technology our kids use at home."

Nick Bilton, technology journalist

aS

"Before the internet, how did people learn other languages? Did they go to other countries and speak to people?"

Kate, age 11

“Yes, kids love technology, but they also love Legos, scented markers, handstands, books, and mud puddles. It’s all about balance.”

K.G., first grade teacher

"We can't jump into rivers anymore because our iPhones will get ruined. We can't take skinny dips in the ocean because there's no service on the beach and adventures aren't real unless they're on Instagram. Technology has doomed the spontaneity of adventure and we're helping destroy it every time we Google, check-in, and hashtag."

Jeremy Glass, author

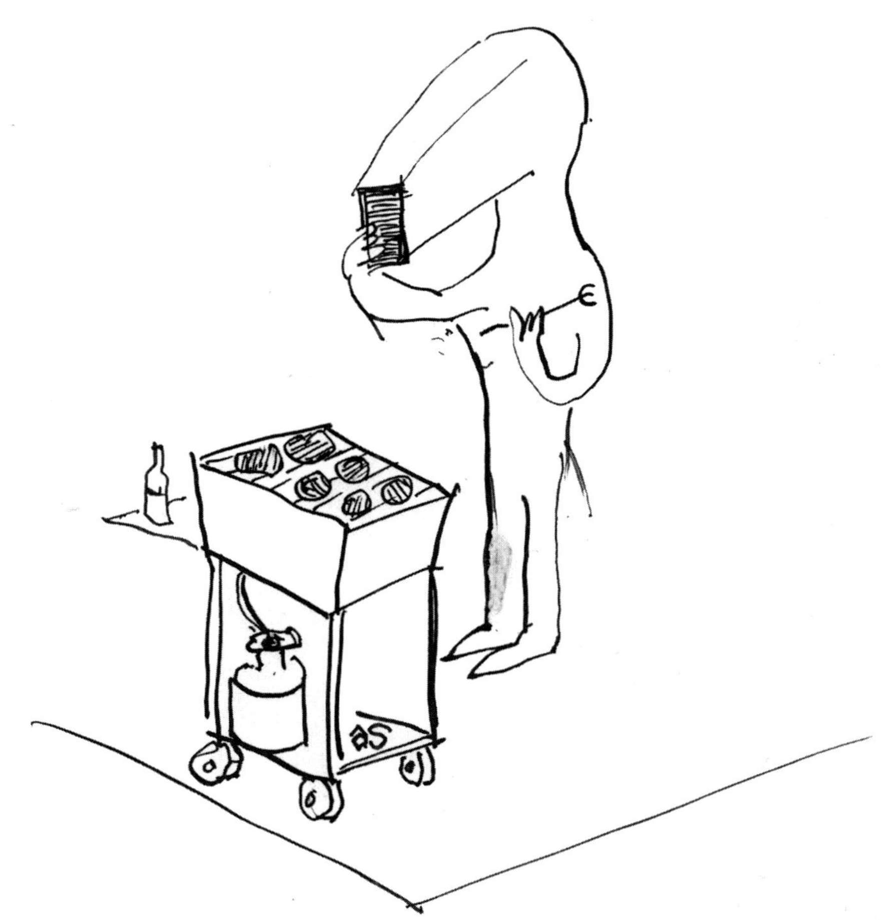

“Fifty percent of teens admit to feeling addicted to their mobile devices.”

2016 Common Sense Media study of 620 teens

"Soon silence will have passed into legend.
Man has turned his back on silence.
Day after day he invents machines and
devices that increase noise and distract
humanity from the essence of life,
contemplation, meditation."

Jean Arp, painter and poet

"Technology provides so many different channels of loneliness. Every time you check your email and don't see a new message, you know that, even though people have the ability to contact you at any time of the day from anywhere on the planet, no one is interested in doing so."

Adi Alsaid, author, in the novel 'Somewhere Over the Sun'

"The true life is not reducible to words spoken or written, not by anyone, ever. The true life takes place when you're alone, thinking, feeling, lost in memory, dreamingly self-aware, the submicroscopic moments."

Don DeLillo, author, in the novel 'Point Omega'

aS

"The present tense made him nervous."

William Gibson, in the novel 'Neuromancer'

aS

“It is possible to be homesick for a place even when you are there.”

Don DeLillo, in the novel ‘White Noise’

aS

“The shower is gap time, and creativity requires gap time. Time for our minds to make subtle connections.”

Joe Kraus, tech sector entrepreneur

"All this modern technology that's supposed to save us time and effort has actually ended up making things more complicated in my life, eating up extra time."

Dean Karnazes, ultramarathon runner

"The problem was too much information.
People were giving up on understanding anything.
The glut of information was dulling awareness, not aiding it.
Overload. It encouraged passivity, not involvement."

Jerry Mander, advertising executive
and author of 'Four Arguments for the Elimination of Television'

"I can see the machine as something that needs to be put down the way an alcoholic puts down drink."

Will Self, author

"When these things first appeared, they were so cool. Only when it was too late did people realize they are as cool as electronic tags on remand prisoners."

David Mitchell, author, in the novel 'Ghostwritten'

"The test of the machine is the satisfaction it gives you. There isn't any other test. If the machine produces tranquility it's right. If it disturbs you it's wrong until either the machine or your mind is changed."

Robert Pirsig, author, in 'Zen and the Art of Motorcycle Maintenance'

“I hate the internet. As I get older I want less of it in my life.”

Ned Beauman, author, born 1985

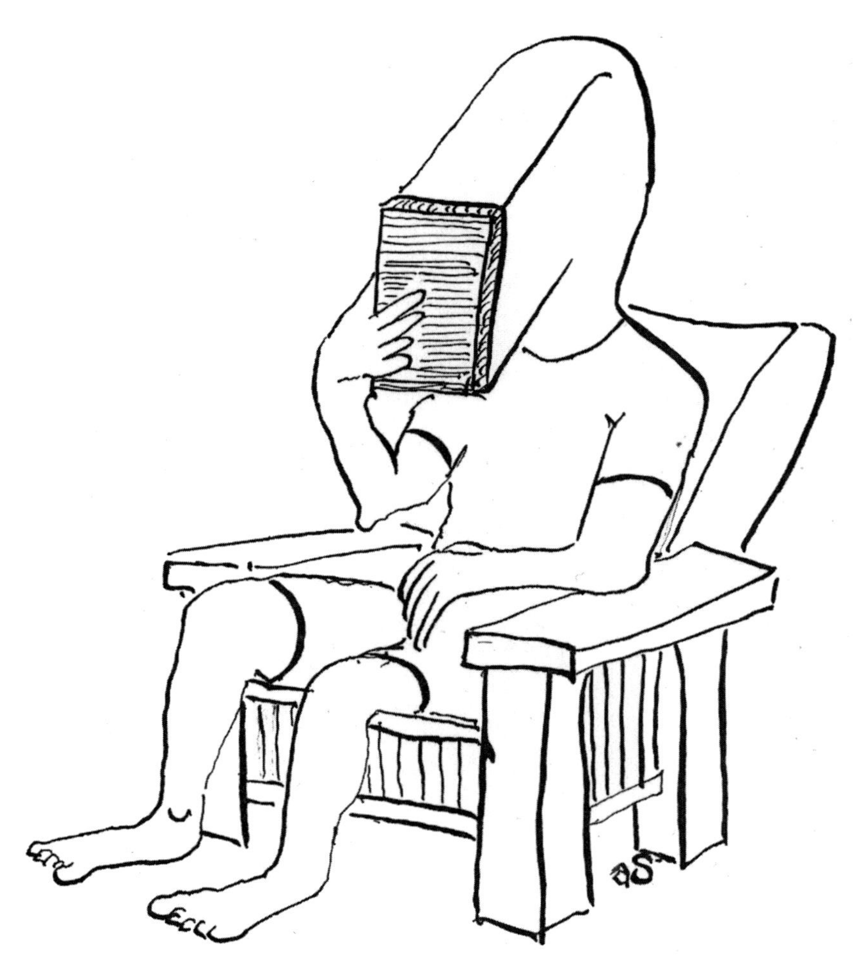

"All of our technology is completely unnecessary to a happy life."

Tom Hodgkinson, author

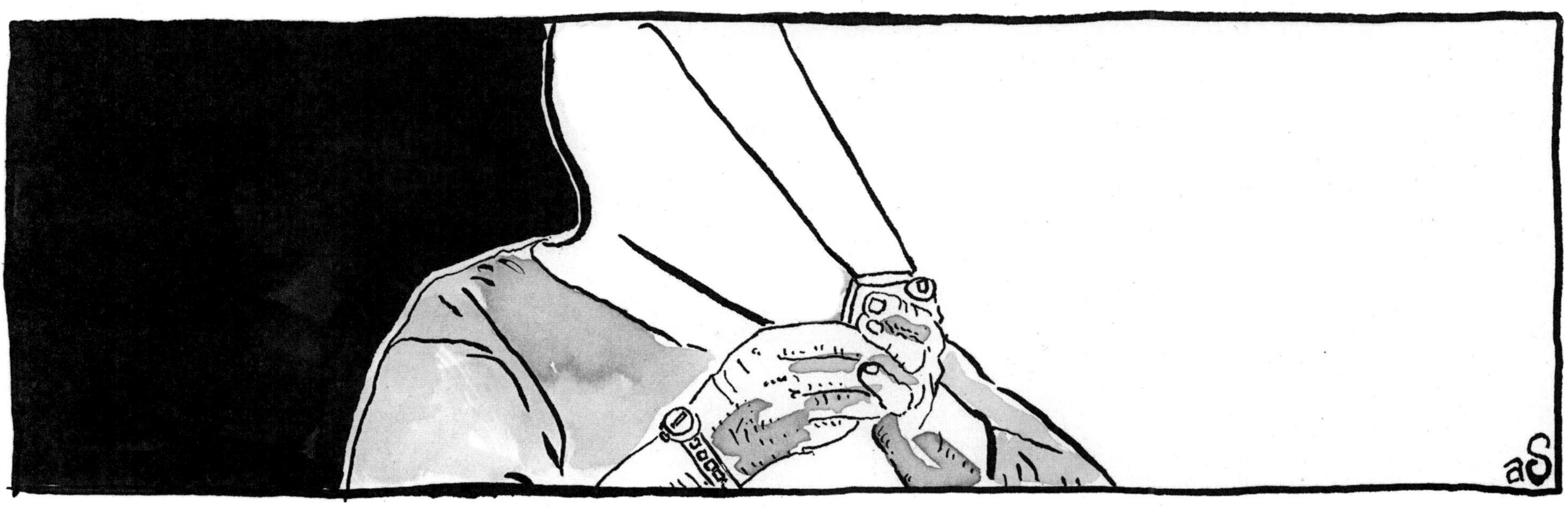

“Flaubert didn’t just hate the railway as such; he hated the way it flattered people with the illusion of progress. What was the point of scientific advance without moral advance? The railway would merely permit more people to move about, meet and be stupid together.”

Julian Barnes, author, in the novel ‘Flaubert’s Parrot’

"Before you become too entranced with gorgeous gadgets
and mesmerizing video displays, let me remind you that
information is not knowledge, knowledge is not wisdom,
and wisdom is not foresight.
Each grows out of the other, and we need them all."

Arthur C. Clarke, author

"We suffer from a poverty of the spirit which stands in glaring contrast to our scientific and technological abundance."

Martin Luther King Jr., religious and political leader

"Our identity is affected less and less by what we produce and more and more by what we consume."

Pete Sanders, counsellor and author

"Men and women are sacrificed
to the idols of profit and consumption:
it is the 'culture of waste.'
If a computer breaks down, it is a tragedy;
but poverty, the needs and dramas of so many people,
end up being considered normal."

Pope Francis

"There were runners who couldn't find their clothes,
who didn't have their phones, who couldn't find their families.
It reminded me how important it is to memorize a few phone numbers."

Kathleen Hunt, volunteer, after the 2013 Boston Marathon bombings

"If you worship money and things,
if they are where you tap real meaning in life,
then you will never have enough,
never feel you have enough.
It's the truth."

David Foster Wallace, author of 'Infinite Jest'

aS·APTER·PS

"Concentrate every minute on doing what's in front of you with precise and genuine seriousness; tenderly, willingly, with justice. And, on freeing yourself from all other distractions, do everything as if it were the last thing you were doing in your life. Stop being aimless."

Marcus Aurelius, Roman emperor and philosopher, in his 'Meditations'

"Men have become the tools of their tools."

Henry Thoreau, author, philosopher, naturalist

“Technology is the knack of so arranging the world that we do not experience it.”

Rollo May, author of ‘The Cry for Myth’

aS

"Computers are useless. They can only give you answers."

Pablo Picasso, artist

“I can’t blame modern technology for my predilection for distraction, not after all the hours I’ve spent watching lost balloons disappear into the clouds.”

Colson Whitehead, author

"We are in great haste to construct a magnetic telegraph from Maine to Texas; but Maine and Texas may have nothing important to communicate."

Henry Thoreau, author, philosopher, naturalist

Life is a brief moment of waking in an eternity of sleep

At One With Two Phones

References (by page number)

6. 'Ed Sheeran quits social media – for now', Maev Kennedy, The Guardian, 13 Dec 2015
8. 'The New Shock of the New', Robert Hughes, Art documentary, BBC television, 2004
10.'Idoru', William Gibson (1996, Viking Press)
12. 'Jazz at the Intergalactic Nightclub', program note, Libby Larsen, 2001.
14. 'Why Putting Down Your Cell Phone Will Help Your Business', Margaret Heffernan, Inc., 26 August, 2013
16. 'Adele tells fan to stop filming gig and enjoy it in real life', The Guardian, 31 May 2016; paraphrased
18. 'Can you connect with me now? How the presence of mobile communication technology influences face-to-face conversation quality', Przybylski, AK, Weinstein, N. J of Social and Personal Relationships, 1-10, July 2012
20. 'Impromptu Scribe' (short stories), Alex Morritt (2014, Paxanax Press)
22. 'Alone Together: Why We Expect More from Technology and Less from Each Other', Sherry Turkle (2011, Basic Books)
24. 'Angels & Demons', Dan Brown (2000, Pocket Books)
26. Rick Taylor, personal correspondence to author, 19 May 2016
28. 'Interview: WALL-E's Andrew Stanton', Mariana McConnell, CinemaBlend, 27 June 2008
30. 'The Circle', David Eggers, (2013, McSweeney's)
32. Susan Greenfield, neuroscientist, as quoted in 'Shutting out a world of digital distraction', Carl Wilkinson, The Telegraph, 6 Sep 2012
34. 'Reflections on the Atom Bomb', Gertrude Stein, (1946), published in Yale Poetry Review, December 1947
36. 'Emma', Jane Austen (1815, John Murray)
38. 'I hate Macs', Charlie Brooker, The Guardian, 5 February 2007
40. 'Meditations', Marcus Aurelius, 170-180 C.E.
42. 'Pope Francis on gay marriage, unmarried mothers ... and journalists', The Guardian, 13 March 2013
44. 'Alone Together: Why We Expect More from Technology and Less from Each Other', Sherry Turkle (2011, Basic Books)
46. Glen Hansard in interview with Brad Frenette, as posted in 'Interview: Glen Hansard finds his rhythm in 'deeper songs', CBC Music blog, 18 June 2012
48. 'To Have or to Be? The Nature of the Psyche', Erich Fromm, 1976
50. 'Slow Tech' (speech), Joe Kraus, TED among Friends, 19 April 2012
52. H. G. Wells, widely attributed, exact source unknown
54. 'Homo Faber', Max Frisch (1957, Abelard-Schuman)
56. 'The Story of Philosophy: The Lives and Opinions of the World's Greatest Philosophers', Will Durant (1926) (1991, Simon & Schuster/Pocket Books)
58. "At The End Of The Mechanical Age", Donald Barthelme, from 'Sixty Stories' (1981, G.P. Putnam's Sons)
60. 'Spielberg in the Twilight Zone', Lisa Kennedy, Wired, 1 June 2002
62. Rosen, L. D., Carrier, L. M., & Cheever, N. A. (2013). Facebook and texting made me do it: Media-induced task-switching while studying. Computers in Human Behavior, 29(3), 948–958.
64. 'William Gibson', Interview with Amy Cavanaugh, A.V. Club, 14 Oct 2011
66. from 'Ten rules for writing fiction', The Guardian, 20 Feb 2010
68. 'Understanding Media: The Extensions of Man', Marshall McLuhan (1964, McGraw-Hill)
70. 'Hollywood's Favorite Cowboy', John Jurgensen, The Wall Street Journal, 20 Nov 2009
72. A.S.
74. 'The New Shock of the New', Robert Hughes, Art documentary, BBC television, 2004
76. 'Calvin and Hobbes' (cartoon strip), Bill Watterson (1985-1995, Andrews McMeel Publishing)
78. 'The AVG 2015 digital diaries', AVG Technologies (2015)
80. 'Technology addiction: Concern, controversy, and finding balance.' Felt, L. J. & Robb, M. B. (2016). San Francisco, CA: Common Sense Media.
82. paraphrasing of quote from 'Interview: Vivienne Westwood: Fashion's pearly queen', Dominic Lutyens, Independent, 7 Nov 1998
84. A.S.
86. 'Steve Jobs Was a Low-Tech Parent', Nick Bilton, New York Times, 10 September, 2014
88. Kate Scamvougeras, during conversation, 2016
90. exact source unknown; identity of K.G. unknown
92. 'We Can't Get Lost Anymore, Jeremy Glass, thoughtcatalog.com, 1 April 2013
94. 'Technology addiction: Concern, controversy, and finding balance.' Felt, L. J. & Robb, M. B. (2016). San Francisco, CA: Common Sense Media.
96. Exact source unknown, widely attributed. (Hans) Jean Arp (1886 –1966), a German-French painter and poet.
98. 'Somewhere Over the Sun', Adi Alsaid (2010, Dog Ear Publishing)
100. 'Point Omega', Don DeLillo (2010, Scribner)
102. 'Neuromancer', William Gibson (1984, Ace)
104. 'White Noise', Don DeLillo (1985, Viking Adult)
106. 'Slow Tech' (speech), Joe Kraus, TED among Friends, 19 April 2012
108. Dean Karnazes, on his Runner's World blog 'Long Running Favourite', 28 January 2013
110. 'Four Arguments for the Elimination of Television', Jerry Mander (1977, William Morrow)
112. Will Self, author, as quoted in 'Shutting out a world of digital distraction', Carl Wilkinson, The Telegraph, 6 Sep 2012
114. 'Ghostwritten', David Mitchell (1999, Hodder & Stoughton)
116. 'Zen and the Art of Motorcycle Maintenance: An Inquiry Into Values', Robert M. Pirsig (1974, William Morrow & Company)
118. Ned Beauman, author, as quoted in 'Shutting out a world of digital distraction', Carl Wilkinson, The Telegraph, 6 Sep 2012
122. 'Shakespeare had no BlackBerry and Aristotle mananged without an iPhone', Tom Hodgkinson, The Guardian, 10 Nov 2009.
124. 'Flaubert's Parrot', Julian Barnes (1984, Jonathan Cape)
126. Arthur C. Clarke, exact source unknown, widely attributed.
128. 'Where Do We Go from Here: Chaos or Community?', Martin Luther King Jr. (1967, HarperCollins)
130. Pete Sanders in 'Politicizing the Person-Centred Approach: An Agenda for Social Change', eds. Proctor G., Cooper M., Sanders P., Malcolm, B. (2006, PCCS Books)
132. Pope Francis, June 5, 2013, general audience, St. Peter's Square
134. Kathleen Hunt as quoted in 'What did you do when the bombs went off?', Jeff Fredrich, Slate, 16 April 2013
136. David Foster Wallace (1962-2008), from 'This Is Water' (transcript of commencement speech given at Kenyon College in 2005), 2009 (Little, Brown and Company)
138. 'Meditations', Marcus Aurelius, 170-180 C.E.
140. 'Walden', Henry Thoreau (1854)
142. 'The Cry for Myth', Rollo May, (1991, W.W. Norton & Company)
144. as quoted in "Pablo Picasso: A Composite Interview", William Fifield, The Paris Review 32, Summer-Fall 1964
146. 'Better Than Renting Out A Windowless Room: The Blessed Distraction Of Technology', Colson Whitehead, Publishers Weekly, 25 April 2011
148. 'Walden', Henry Thoreau (1854)
150. 'Life is a brief moment of waking in an eternity of sleep'. Exact source unclear; can't find it online. I used it in a 2006 project; possibly my own composite. Any light shed on this appreciated. - AS

Titles of Illustrations (by page number)

The artist has exercised the right to create parodies of existing works.

Phone Facts

Earth's population: 7.4 billion people
People with access to mobile phones: 6 billion [1]
People with access to working toilets: 4.5 billion [1]
The number of active mobile devices and human beings crossed at 7.19 billion, in 2014 [2]
Mobile devices are multiplying five times faster than humans [2]

64% of Americans own a smartphone [3]
Smartphone owners spend an average of 2 hours per day using their phones [4]
46% of American cell phone owners say that it is something they "couldn't live without" [3]
95% of smartphone users have used their phones during social gatherings [4]
70% have used their phones while working [4]
93% of smartphone owners use their phones to avoid being bored [3]
47% use their phone to avoid interacting with the people around them [3]
35% check the web before getting out of bed [19]
10% admitted to checking their phones during sex [4]

57% reported feeling "distracted" thanks to their phone [3]
36% reported that their phone made them feel "frustrated" [3]

54% of children felt that their parents checked their devices too often [5]
77% of parents feel their teens get distracted by devices [6]
41% of teens feel their parents get distracted by devices [6]

Teens watch TV (51%), use social media (50%), and text (60%) while doing homework [7]
Most teens do not feel that multitasking harms the quality of their work [7]
59% of parents of 0-8 yr olds said they were not worried about their children becoming addicted to new interactive technologies [9]

1. 'More People Have Cell Phones Than Toilets, U.N. Study Shows', Yue Wang, TIME, 25 March 2013
2. 'There are officially more mobile devices than people in the world', Zachary Davies Boren, The Independent, 7 October 2014
3. 'The Smartphone Difference', Pew Research Center, April, 2015
4. 'Study: Smartphone alerts increase inattention - and hyperactivity', Fariss Samarrai, UVA Today, University of Virginia, 9 May 2016
5. 'The AVG 2015 digital diaries', AVG Technologies. (2015).
6. Felt, L. J. & Robb, M. B. (2016). Technology addiction: Concern, controversy, and finding balance. San Francisco, CA: Common Sense Media.
7. Common Sense Media. (2015). The Common Sense census: Media use by tweens and teens. San Francisco, CA: Common Sense Media.
8. Radesky, J. S., et al. (2014). Patterns of mobile device use by caregivers and children during meals in fast food restaurants. Pediatrics, 133(4), e843–e849.
9. Wartella, E., Rideout, V., Lauricella, A. & Connell, S. (2013). Parenting in the Age of Digital Technology. Report for the Center on Media and Human Development School of Communication Northwestern University.
10. Common Sense Media. (2012). Social media, social life: How teens view their digital lives. San Francisco, CA: Common Sense Media.
11. 'Cellphone use causes over 1 in 4 car accidents', Gabrielle Kratas, USA Today, 28 March 2014
12. 'Impact of social and technological distraction on pedestrian crossing behaviour: an observational study', L.L.Thompson et al, Inj Prev 2013;19:232-237

Parents who were highly absorbed in their devices tended to be more harsh when dealing with their child's misbehaviour [8]
Children between the ages of 13 and 17 preferred face-to-face communication over all technological means of communication, because it was perceived to be more fun and because they could understand people better in person [10]

The U.S. National Safety Council found that the use of cell phones causes 26% of U.S. car accidents [11]
Reaching for a cellphone, dialing, or texting while driving increases crash risk by a factor of three [17]

30% of US pedestrians use distracting personal technology while crossing at high-risk intersections [12]
After a 15-year old girl was killed by a tram while texting, the city of Augsburg, Germany, installed traffic lights embedded in the pavement designed to alert pedestrians looking down at their phones [14]
A pedestrian sidewalk lane reserved for heavy users of mobile devices, in the city of Chongqing, China, appears to have failed because most cell-phone users didn't notice the new lane [15]
A 20-foot tall sculpture, 'The Kiss', by Sophie Ryder, depicting two clasped hands, had to be moved from its position arching over a path near Salisbury Cathedral, England, because people distracted by their cell-phones were walking into it [16]

Students experience significantly higher levels of inattention and hyperactivity when smartphone alerts were turned on [4]
Students demonstrated reduced motor task abilities when their own or another person's cell phone was visible to them [13]
Students in a lecture who were not using their mobile phones wrote down 62% more information in notes, took more detailed notes, were able to recall more detailed information, and scored a full letter grade and a half higher on a multiple choice test than those students who were actively using their mobile phones [18]
Number of texts sent or received by an average 13-17 yr old girl, in a month, in 2012: 4000 (ave. one every 7 min.) [19]

High frequency of mobile phone use is associated with disturbed sleep [20]
The longer a teenager spent looking at an electronic screen before going to bed, the worse quality sleep they were likely to have [21]
'Text-neck' or 'tech-neck' is a condition that results from constantly looking down at handheld technology [22]
In a London study, cases of near-sightedness have risen 35 percent since the advent of smartphones [22]
Too much screen time can lead to dry eyes. "It causes a decreased blink rate. People just aren't blinking enough." [22]

13. 'How Your Cell Phone Distracts You Even When You're Not Using It', Justin Worland, TIME, 4 December, 2014
14. 'This city embedded traffic lights in the sidewalks so that smartphone users don't have to look up', Rick Noack, Washington Post, 25 April 2016
15. 'A Chinese city is asking smartphone users to walk in their own sidewalk lane', Rick Noack, Washington Post, 15 Sept 2014
16. 'Put away your phone and enjoy the world around you', Michael Henderson, The Telegraph, 21 February, 2016
17. Fitch, G. A. et al. (2013, April). The impact of hand-held and hands-free cell phone use on driving performance and safety-critical event risk. Washington, DC: National Highway Traffic Safety Administration
18. Kuznekoff. J. H. and Titsworth, S. (2013). The impact of mobile phone usage on student learning. Communication Education, 62 (3), 233-252.
19. Joe Kraus speech, 'Slow Tech', TED among Friends, 19 April 2012
20. 'ICT use and mental health in young adults', Sara Thomée (2012, University of Gothenburg Press)
21. 'Too much exposure to smartphone screens ruins your sleep', Charlie Cooper, Independent, 2 Feb 2015
22. 'Techitis: Constantly using Smartphones Causing Widespread Health Problems', Kym Gable, CBS Pittsburgh, 19 May 2016